SCHOLASTIC

D0471835

Practice, Practice, Practice!

ALGEBRA READINESS

by Judith A. Muschla
and
Gary Robert Muschla

New York • Toronto • London • Auckland • Sydney
Mexico City • New Delhi • Hong Kong • Buenos Aires

Teaching *Resources*

Dedication

For Erin

Cover design by Maria Lilja

Interior design by Ellen Matlach for Boultinghouse & Boultinghouse, Inc.

Interior illustrations by Teresa Anderko

ISBN: 0-439-52961-1

Contents

Introduction

In recent years pre-algebra has emerged as a major topic in elementary and middle school mathematics. Not only does pre-algebra prepare students for the study of traditional algebra, it also fosters a student's problem-solving skills, promotes the ability to express mathematical relationships, and extends a student's overall proficiency in math.

The purpose of *Practice, Practice, Practice! Algebra Readiness* is threefold:

- To provide students with reproducible activities that will help them to master the skills and concepts of pre-algebra.

- To provide students with activities that support the standards of the NCTM and that serve as a foundation for the skills and concepts found in the typical algebra curriculum.

- To provide students with activities that are motivating, challenging, and fun.

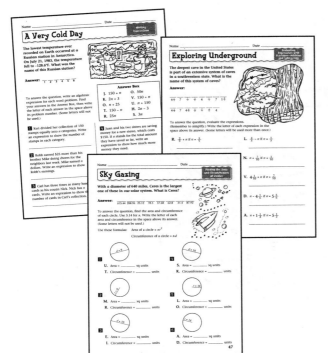

What This Book Contains

This book contains 52 reproducible activities that focus on the skills and concepts of pre-algebra. The activities progress from basic to challenging and are designed to meet the needs of math students in grades 4 through 8. The book begins with finding basic patterns and advances through all of the major skills associated with pre-algebra, including writing expressions, using the order of operations, evaluating expressions, writing equations, solving equations, working with formulas, finding equalities and inequalities, and graphing ordered pairs. The activities require students to work with whole numbers, fractions, decimals, percents, and integers.

All of the activities are self-correcting. Students are presented with a question at the beginning of each activity, which they can answer by correctly solving the problems. For most of the activities, a few problems that do not help to answer the questions are included to make the activities more challenging. The questions that begin the activities are derived from various subjects, including geography, history, science, literature, ecology, and pop culture.

An answer key is included at the end of the book. The key shows the answers to each problem as well as the answers to the puzzles.

How to Use This Book

Each activity in this book stands alone and may be used in a manner that best satisfies the needs of your students. You may use the activities in various ways: to supplement your instruction, for reinforcement, for extra credit, for challenges, or for substitute plans.

The activities are designed for easy implementation. Each is reproducible, has easy-to-follow instructions, and requires no additional materials. While a few activities, for example, "A Ride in Space" (finding the square root of a number), are best completed using calculators, the use of calculators for most activities is optional. You may encourage students to utilize calculators for computation, or you may instruct them to work problems out for practice.

While the titles of the activities are related to the questions, the specific skill(s) each activity addresses is noted at the top of the page. These skills are also included in the table of contents beneath the title. Thus, the contents functions as a skills list, making it easy for you to identify the activities that will be of most benefit to your students.

Connections to the NCTM Principles and Standards

All of the activities in this book align with the *NCTM's Principles and Standards for School Mathematics*. While the activities concentrate on skills and concepts that are essential to pre-algebra curricula, development of mathematical skills and reasoning are also encouraged throughout the book.

We trust that your students will enjoy these activities and that you will find the activities to be a positive supplement to your math program. We wish you well in your teaching.

Judith A. Muschla
Gary Robert Muschla

Name _____   Date _____

The First Dinosaur

Dinosaurs ruled Earth for about 180 million years, until they died out 65 million years ago. Many historians agree that an Englishwoman, Mary Mantell, discovered the first dinosaur bones in 1822. What was this dinosaur named?

Answer: $\underset{1}{\text{I}}$ $\underset{2}{\quad}$ $\underset{3}{\quad}$ $\underset{4}{\quad}$ $\underset{5}{\quad}$ $\underset{6}{\quad}$ $\underset{7}{\quad}$ $\underset{8}{\quad}$ $\underset{9}{\quad}$

To answer the question, complete each pattern. Find the last answer of each pattern in the Answer Box, then write the letter of the answer in the space above its problem number. (Some letters will not be used.)

1 1, 3, 5, 7, __9__, __11__, __13__

2 2, 4, 8, 16, _____, _____, _____

3 30, 29, 27, 24, _____, _____, _____

4 1, 6, 11, 16, _____, _____, _____

5 7, 8, 10, 13, _____, _____, _____

6 729, 243, 81, 27, _____, _____, _____

7 ●, ★, ●●, ★★, _____, _____, _____

8 ★●, ★★●, ★★●●, ★★★●●, _____,
_____, _____

9 ★, ★●, ★★, ★★●●, _____,
_____, _____

Answer Box
C. 14
S. ★★★★★
N. 28
R. 12
D. ●●●●
H. 192
A. 31
V. ★●★●★●
I. 13
U. 9
O. 1
N. ★★★★
G. 128
O. ★★★★●●●●
M. 22

Lady Inventor

The first patent granted to a woman in the United States was for a machine that weaved straw with silk or thread. The year was 1809. What was this woman's name?

Answer: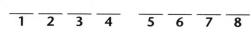
1   2   3   4   5   6   7   8

To answer the question, complete each pattern. Find the last answer of each pattern in the Answer Box, then write the letter of the answer in the space above its problem number. (Some letters will not be used.)

Answer Box
I. 2.5
B. 1
W. ★★★●
T. 2.3
N. 2
D. 2.55
Y. 21
R. ★★★
H. ●●●●
K. ●●●●●
E. 64
S. $\frac{3}{10}$
M. 24
J. 81
A. ★★★★
L. $\frac{1}{5}$

1 6, 9, 12, 15, _____, _____, _____

2 ★, ●●, ★★, ●●●, _____, _____, _____

3 ★, ●, ★●, ★★, _____, _____, _____

4 1, 1, 2, 3, 5, _____, _____, _____

5 ●●, ★, ●●●, ★★, _____, _____, _____

6 1, 1.25, 1.5, 1.75, _____, _____, _____

7 4, 9, 16, 25, _____, _____, _____

8 $\frac{9}{10}$, $\frac{4}{5}$, $\frac{7}{10}$, $\frac{3}{5}$, _____, _____, _____

Practice, Practice, Practice! Algebra Readiness Scholastic Teaching Resources

Name _____ Date _____

"Happy Birthday to You"

Just about everybody knows the song "Happy Birthday to You." Composed in 1893, it has been sung at birthday parties for more than 100 years. Two sisters wrote the song. Who were they?

Answer:

$$\overline{18} \ \overline{15} \ \overline{41} \ \overline{69} \ \overline{8} \ \overline{11} \ \overline{69} \quad \overline{31} \ \overline{146} \ \overline{69}$$

$$\overline{19} \ \overline{31} \ \overline{72} \ \overline{72} \ \overline{7} \quad \overline{6} \ \overline{15} \ \overline{41} \ \overline{41}$$

To answer the question, solve the equations. Write the letter of the problem in the space above its answer. (Some letters will be used more than once. Some letters will not be used.)

E. $8 + n = 19$

$n =$ _____

P. $n - 7 = 12$

$n =$ _____

N. $101 = n - 45$

$n =$ _____

A. $n + 12 = 43$

$n =$ _____

D. $56 = n - 13$

$n =$ _____

I. $n + 14 = 29$

$n =$ _____

U. $n - 8 = 8$

$n =$ _____

H. $n = 82 - 76$

$n =$ _____

K. $n = 324 - 192$

$n =$ _____

R. $26 + n = 34$

$n =$ _____

M. $92 + n = 110$

$n =$ _____

T. $n - 18 = 54$

$n =$ _____

S. $n - 32 = 51$

$n =$ _____

L. $17 + n = 58$

$n =$ _____

Y. $n + 65 = 72$

$n =$ _____

Practice, Practice, Practice! Algebra Readiness   Scholastic Teaching Resources

9

Name _____   Date _____

Uncle Sam

Most people are familiar with the image of "Uncle Sam." With his white hair and top hat, he is a symbol of the United States. The artist who drew the picture used himself as a model. Who was this artist?

Answer:

$$\overline{\text{168}} \; \overline{\text{6}} \; \overline{\text{12}} \; \overline{\text{125}} \; \overline{\text{84}}$$

$$\overline{\text{12}} \; \overline{\text{33}} \; \overline{\text{243}} \; \overline{\text{7}} \; \overline{\text{144}} \; \overline{\text{33}} \; \overline{\text{12}} \; \overline{\text{125}} \; \overline{\text{3}} \; \overline{\text{147}}$$

$$\overline{\text{5}} \; \overline{\text{2}} \; \overline{\text{6}} \; \overline{\text{144}} \; \overline{\text{144}}$$

To answer the question, solve the equations. Write the letter of the problem in the space above its answer. (Some letters will be used more than once. Some letters will not be used.)

L. $7 \times n = 14$

n = _____

M. $n \times 6 = 72$

n = _____

Y. $n \div 7 = 21$

n = _____

T. $n \times 9 = 63$

n = _____

N. $n \div 3 = 81$

n = _____

A. $64 \times n = 384$

n = _____

R. $14 \times n = 42$

n = _____

H. $n \div 5 = 73$

n = _____

O. $n \times 11 = 363$

n = _____

U. $n \div 8 = 9$

n = _____

F. $84 \times n = 420$

n = _____

G. $n \div 12 = 12$

n = _____

E. $n \div 25 = 5$

n = _____

S. $n \div 7 = 12$

n = _____

J. $n \div 2 = 84$

n = _____

Practice, Practice, Practice! Algebra Readiness   Scholastic Teaching Resources

Wild Weather

On January 22, 1943, one of the most extreme changes in temperature ever recorded happened in the United States. At 7:30 A.M., the temperature was −4°F. Within the next two minutes, it rose 49° to 45°F. Where did this rapid temperature change occur?

Answer:

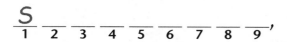

$\dfrac{S}{1}$ $\dfrac{}{2}$ $\dfrac{}{3}$ $\dfrac{}{4}$ $\dfrac{}{5}$ $\dfrac{}{6}$ $\dfrac{}{7}$ $\dfrac{}{8}$ $\dfrac{}{9}$,

$\dfrac{}{10}$ $\dfrac{}{11}$ $\dfrac{}{12}$ $\dfrac{}{13}$ $\dfrac{}{14}$ $\dfrac{}{15}$ $\dfrac{}{16}$ $\dfrac{}{17}$ $\dfrac{}{18}$ $\dfrac{}{19}$ $\dfrac{}{20}$

To answer the question, complete the function tables. Match your answers with the answers in the Answer Box, then write the letter of each answer in the space above its problem number. The first one has been done for you.

I. $y = 5x$

x	1	2	3
y	5		

   1   2   3

II. $y = 2x + 2$

x	0	1	3
y			

   4   5   6

III. $y = 8x - 2$

x	1	2	4
y			

   7   8   9

IV. $y = 2x + 3$

x	5	10	15
y			

   10   11   12

V. $y = 5x - 4$

x	4	5	6	7
y				

   13   14   15   16

VI. $y = 9 + 3x$

x	3	6	9	12
y				

   17   18   19   20

Answer Box

E. 15	O. 23
H. 21	A. 2
S. 5	U. 33
H. 30	P. 10
F. 8	A. 31
S. 13	I. 6
A. 45	K. 18
R. 4	O. 27
D. 26	S. 14
T. 36	T. 16

A Speedy Flyer

The fastest bird in the world can fly
at speeds up to 106 miles per hour.
What is the name of this speedy bird?

Answer:

$$\overline{4}\;\overline{56}\;\overline{29}\;\overline{66}\;\overline{336}\;\overset{-}{\overline{5}}\;\overline{6}\;\overline{29}\;\overline{54}\;\overline{336}\;\overline{140}$$

$$\overline{4}\;\overline{72}\;\overline{29}\;\overline{147}\;\overline{5}$$

To answer the question, solve the equations. Write the letter
of the problem in the space above its answer. (Some letters
will be used more than once. Some letters will not be used.)

L. $n - 19 = 35$

$n =$ _____

N. $n + 38 = 104$

$n =$ _____

E. $n \div 8 = 42$

$n =$ _____

U. $15 + n = 23$

$n =$ _____

J. $n - 74 = 25$

$n =$ _____

R. $15 \times n = 105$

$n =$ _____

P. $n \div 8 = 7$

$n =$ _____

S. $n \times 16 = 64$

$n =$ _____

C. $n + 17 = 44$

$n =$ _____

A. $14 \times n = 84$

$n =$ _____

D. $n - 38 = 102$

$n =$ _____

W. $n \div 12 = 6$

$n =$ _____

F. $n \div 21 = 7$

$n =$ _____

I. $81 + n = 110$

$n =$ _____

T. $n \times 28 = 140$

$n =$ _____

Practice, Practice, Practice! Algebra Readiness   Scholastic Teaching Resources

Follow the Signs

The largest active volcano in the world is located in Hawaii. What is the name of this volcano?

Answer:

M ___ ___ ___ ___ ___ ___ ___
1 2   3   4   5   6   7   8

To answer the question, write +, −, ×, or ÷ to make each number sentence true. Then write the letter of the sign in the space above the number of each problem. The first one has been done for you.

1 $2 \times 3 = 13$ ___ 7

   +   −   ×   ÷
   R   (M)   E   S

5 $24 \div 3 = 16$ ___ 8

   +   −   ×   ÷
   Y   A   L   P

2 $9 + 7 = 2$ ___ 8

   +   −   ×   ÷
   B   H   A   I

6 64 ___ $8 = 4 \times 2$

   +   −   ×   ÷
   S   M   F   L

3 4 ___ $9 = 6 \times 6$

   +   −   ×   ÷
   G   A   U   R

7 $15 + 3 = 24$ ___ 6

   +   −   ×   ÷
   E   O   D   W

4 8 ___ $4 = 24 \div 2$

   +   −   ×   ÷÷
   N   S   V   A

8 4 ___ $7 = 14 \times 2$

   +   −   ×   ÷
   R   Q   A   E

A Capital Idea

Washington, D.C., was not always the capital of the United States. From 1790 to 1800, another city was the capital of the country. What city was this?

Answer:

$$\overline{}\ \overline{}\ \overline{}\ \overline{}\ \overline{}\ \overline{}\ \overline{}\ \overline{}\ \overline{}\ \overline{}\ \overline{}\ \overline{}$$

$n-4$ $3n-1$ $n-6$ $n+8$ $n+3$ $2n+1$ $n\div4$ $n+8$ $n-4$ $3n-1$ $n-6$ $n+3$

To answer the question, write an expression for each description. Write the letter of the problem in the space above its answer. (Some letters will be used more than once. Some letters will not be used.)

A. the sum of a number and 3 _____

I. 6 less than a number _____

S. two times a number _____

L. 8 more than a number _____

M. a number minus 5 _____

E. a number divided by 4 _____

D. 1 more than two times a number _____

C. 7 less than four times a number _____

P. 4 less than a number _____

H. 1 less than three times a number _____

Practice, Practice, Practice! Algebra Readiness Scholastic Teaching Resources

Name _____ Date _____

A Very Cold Day

The lowest temperature ever recorded on Earth occurred at a Russian station in Antarctica. On July 21, 1983, the temperature fell to –128.6°F. What was the name of this Russian station?

Answer: $\underline{\hspace{1em}}$ $\underline{\hspace{1em}}$ $\underline{\hspace{1em}}$ $\underline{\hspace{1em}}$ $\underline{\hspace{1em}}$ $\underline{\hspace{1em}}$
　　　　　　1　2　3　4　5　6

To answer the question, write an algebraic expression for each word problem. Find your answers in the Answer Box, then write the letter of each answer in the space above its problem number. (Some letters will not be used.)

Answer Box	
J. $150 + n$	O. $50n$
K. $2n + 3$	V. $150 \div n$
O. $n + 25$	U. $n \div 150$
T. $150 - n$	H. $2n - 3$
R. $25n$	S. $3n$

1 Keri divided her collection of 150 stamps equally into n categories. Write an expression to show the number of stamps in each category.

_____

2 Robb earned $25 more than his brother Mike doing chores for the neighbors last week. Mike earned n dollars. Write an expression to show Robb's earnings.

_____

3 Carl has three times as many baseball cards as his cousin Nick. Nick has n cards. Write an expression to show the number of cards in Carl's collection.

_____

4 Juan and his two sisters are saving money for a new stereo, which costs $150. If n stands for the total amount they have saved so far, write an expression to show how much more money they need.

_____

5 The speed limit on the highway is 50 miles per hour. Write an expression to show the distance traveled in n hours.

_____

6 Let n be any number. Write an expression that is three more than twice that number.

_____

Practice, Practice, Practice! Algebra Readiness　Scholastic Teaching Resources

15

Time for Fun

The oldest amusement park in the United States dates back to 1846 in Bristol, Connecticut. What is the name of this amusement park?

Answer:

$$\overline{\quad}\ \overline{\quad}\ \overline{\quad}\ \overline{\quad}$$
20 35 15 11

$$\overline{\quad}\ \overline{\quad}\ \overline{\quad}\ \overline{\quad}\ \overline{\quad}\ \overline{\quad}\ \overline{\quad}\ \overline{\quad}\ \overline{\quad}$$
0   40 21   6   40 10 33   0   11

To answer the question, solve the following equations. Write the letter of each equation in the space above its answer. (Some letters will be used more than once. Some letters will not be used.)

E. $3(4 + 1) - 4 =$ _____

A. $5(6 - 3) + 2(2 + 8) \div (6 - 5) =$ _____

M. $6(3 + 4) \div 2 =$ _____

O. $3(2 + 6) + 4(7 - 3) =$ _____

N. $3 + 6(2 + 3) =$ _____

R. $(14 \div 2) - (6 - 2) =$ _____

K. $2(12 \div 3) + 7 =$ _____

U. $4(2 + 3) \div (4 - 2) =$ _____

C. $2(12 \div 3) - 8 =$ _____

S. $8(4 + 2) \div (2 \times 6) =$ _____

L. $9 - (3 - 2) + (3 \times 4) =$ _____

P. $2 + 7 - (8 \div 4) - 1 =$ _____

Practice, Practice, Practice! Algebra Readiness   Scholastic Teaching Resources

Iced Tea, Please

When no one would buy his hot tea at the St. Louis World's Fair in 1904 because the weather was too hot, this Englishman added ice to his tea. His new drink proved to be very popular then and remains popular today. Who was he?

Answer:

$$\overline{12}\ \overline{10}\ \overline{8}\ \overline{7}\ \overline{4}\ \overline{12}\ \overline{11}\quad \overline{1}\ \overline{6}\ \overline{2}\ \overline{8}\ \overline{7}\ \overline{5}\ \overline{3}\ \overline{11}\ \overline{2}\quad \overline{3}$$

To answer the question, complete each equation by supplying the missing number. Write the letter of each equation in the space above the number that completes it. (Some letters will be used more than once. One letter will not be used.)

L. $(2 + \underline{\hspace{1cm}}) \times (3 - 1) = 16$

I. $\underline{\hspace{1cm}} - (4 \times 2) + (6 - 2) = 6$

Y. $\underline{\hspace{1cm}}(5 - 2) = 15$

C. $32 \div \underline{\hspace{1cm}} + 3(7 + 2) = 31$

A. $(32 \div 4) - (2 \times \underline{\hspace{1cm}}) = 0$

R. $(27 - 11) \div 2(\underline{\hspace{1cm}} - 10) = 4$

N. $\underline{\hspace{1cm}}(6 + 2) \div (6 - 3) = 8$

D. $4(\underline{\hspace{1cm}} - 5) \times 2(5 - 4) = 48$

H. $9 + (\underline{\hspace{1cm}} \times 2) - 6 = 17$

S. $4(3 - 1) + 5(\underline{\hspace{1cm}} - 7) = 38$

E. $3(25 \div 5) + (8 \div \underline{\hspace{1cm}}) = 19$

B. $3(14 - 6) + 8(6 - \underline{\hspace{1cm}}) \div (16 \div 2) = 8$

Watch Your Step

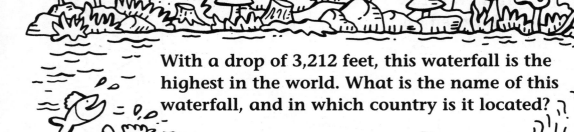

With a drop of 3,212 feet, this waterfall is the highest in the world. What is the name of this waterfall, and in which country is it located?

To answer the question, evaluate each expression for $n = 3$, $t = 5$, and $y = 7$. Then write the letter of the expression in the space above its answer. (Some letters will be used more than once. Some letters will not be used.) The first one has been done for you.

$$\overline{}\ \overline{}\ \overline{}\ \overline{}\ \overline{}\quad \overline{}\ \overline{}\ \overline{}\ \overline{}\ \overline{},$$

| 4 | 120 | 30 | 26 | 8 | | 42 | 4 | 8 | 8 | 56 |

$$\underset{\text{U}}{\overline{}}$$

| 13 | 26 | 120 | 26 | 12 | 18 | 26 | 8 | 4 |

U. $6 \times n$ _____18_____

B. $(n + t) \div 4$ _____

L. $24 \div n$ _____

W. $(18 \div n) \div 2$ _____

N. $10 \times (y + t)$ _____

H. $75 \div (n \times t)$ _____

E. $(t \times n) + (y + 4)$ _____

J. $(y + 8) - (t - 4)$ _____

R. $t + y + 4$ _____

A. $14 - (n + y)$ _____

T. $t \times 4 - n$ _____

F. $2 \times (n \times y)$ _____

S. $8 \times y$ _____

V. $(70 \div y) + n$ _____

G. $45 - (n \times t)$ _____

Z. $24 \div (y - t)$ _____

Practice, Practice, Practice! Algebra Readiness   Scholastic Teaching Resources

A Famous Author

C. S. Lewis is well known as the author of
the series Chronicles of Narnia. Less well
known is his full name. What do the
initials *C. S.* stand for?

Answer:

$$\overline{\hspace{1cm}} \quad \overline{\hspace{1cm}} \quad \overline{\hspace{1cm}} \quad \overline{\hspace{1cm}} \quad \overline{\hspace{1cm}}$$
$5n - 6 = 9 \quad n \div 8 = 9 \quad n(2 + 1) = 9 \quad n + 4 = 9 \quad 3(n + 1) = 9$

$$\overline{\hspace{1cm}} \quad \overline{\hspace{1cm}} \quad \overline{\hspace{1cm}} \quad \overline{\hspace{1cm}} \quad \overline{\hspace{1cm}} \quad \overline{\hspace{1cm}} \quad \overline{\hspace{1cm}}$$
$(3n + 3) \div 3 \quad n - 4 = 9 \quad 3n - 3 = 9 \quad n \div 2 + 5 \quad n \div 8 = 9 \quad 3(n + 1) = 9 \quad (3n + 3) \div 3$
$= 9 \hspace{3.5cm} = 9 \hspace{5.5cm} = 9$

To answer the question, write an algebraic equation for each sentence.
Write the letter of each problem in the space above its equation. (Some
letters will be used more than once. Some letters will not be used.)

V. 4 more than *n* is 9. _____

T. 4 less than *n* is 9. _____

L. *n* divided by 8 is 9. _____

R. 3 times *n* is 9. _____

P. 5 more than *n* divided by 2 is 9. _____

C. 6 less than 5 times *n* is 9. _____

N. *n* times 3 divided by 4 is 9. _____

A. 3 times *n* minus 3 is 9. _____

H. the sum of *n* and 4 divided by 2 is 9. _____

E. 3 times the sum of *n* and 1 is 9. _____

S. the sum of 3 times *n* plus 3 divided by 3 is 9. _____

I. *n* times the sum of 2 and 1 is 9. _____

A Sticky Situation

In 1955, George D. Mestral invented a product that most Americans since then have used at one time or another. What is this product?

Answer:

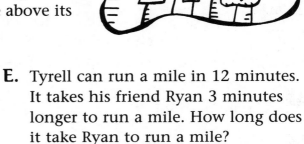

$3 \times 12 = n$	$12 + 3 = n$	$16 - 12 = n$	$12 \div 3 = n$	$36 \div 3 = n$	$12 - 4 = n$

To answer the question, write an equation for each problem. Then write the letter of the problem in the space above its equation. Let n stand for the missing numbers.

L. Joe had to complete 12 math problems for homework. He copied his assignment incorrectly and completed 16 problems. How many extra problems did he do?

_____

O. Mike lost some of the pieces of his checkers set. He now has only 12 pieces, including 4 four red ones. How many black pieces does he have?

_____

R. Marie and her two cousins are planning refreshments for a family gathering. They need 3 dozen cupcakes. How many cupcakes should each girl bake if they are to bake the same amount?

_____

E. Tyrell can run a mile in 12 minutes. It takes his friend Ryan 3 minutes longer to run a mile. How long does it take Ryan to run a mile?

_____

C. Danielle is selling wrapping paper to raise money for her class. The class will reach its goal if everyone sells 12 rolls. Danielle plans to reach this goal if she sells 3 rolls of paper per day. How many days will it take her to sell the wrapping paper?

_____

V. Marina is helping her teacher by cutting out circles for a class activity. There are three groups of students and each group needs a dozen circles. How many circles does Marina need to make?

_____

Practice, Practice, Practice! Algebra Readiness Scholastic Teaching Resources

Name _____   Date _____

A Big Group

The largest of all animal groups includes insects, arachnids (spiders), and crustaceans (lobsters and shrimp). What is the name of this animal group?

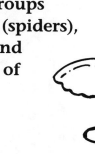

Answer:

‾‾ ‾‾ ‾‾ ‾‾ ‾‾ ‾‾ ‾‾ ‾‾ ‾‾ ‾‾
1   2   3   4   5   6   7   8   9   10

To answer the question, match the equations with the properties they demonstrate. Write the letter of the property in the space above the equation number.

1 $7 \times 0 = 0$ _____

2 $(7 \times 3) \times 4 = 7 \times (3 \times 4)$ _____

3 $21 + 8 = 8 + 21$ _____

4 $10 \times 1 = 10$ _____

5 $(9 \times 6) \times 2 = 9 \times (6 \times 2)$ _____

6 $3 \times 5 = 5 \times 3$ _____

7 $(3 + 9) + 4 = 3 + (9 + 4)$ _____

8 $106 \times 4 = 4 \times 106$ _____

9 $12 + 0 = 12$ _____

10 $9 \times (4 + 8) = (9 \times 4) + (9 \times 8)$ _____

Properties

T. Commutative Property of Addition

P. Associative Property of Addition

D. Zero Property of Addition

A. Zero Property of Multiplication

O. Commutative Property of Multiplication

R. Associative Property of Multiplication

S. Distributive Property

H. Property of One

Practice, Practice, Practice! Algebra Readiness   Scholastic Teaching Resources

21

Name _____   Date _____

Ice Cream Cones

Ice cream cones have been popular for about a hundred years. The first patent to produce ice cream cones was granted in 1904. To whom was this patent granted?

Answer:

$\overline{\hspace{0.6cm}}$ $\overline{\hspace{0.6cm}}$ $\overline{\hspace{0.6cm}}$ $\overline{\hspace{0.6cm}}$ $\overline{\hspace{0.6cm}}$
4.57 7.21 2.03 1.9 8.23

$\overline{\hspace{0.6cm}}$ $\overline{\hspace{0.6cm}}$ $\overline{\hspace{0.6cm}}$ $\overline{\hspace{0.6cm}}$ $\overline{\hspace{0.6cm}}$ $\overline{\hspace{0.6cm}}$ $\overline{\hspace{0.6cm}}$ $\overline{\hspace{0.6cm}}$ $\overline{\hspace{0.6cm}}$
0.899 2.03 0.7 1.63 2.15 4.57 8.23 8.8 3.28

To answer the question, evaluate the expressions. Write the letter of each expression in the space above its answer. (Some letters will be used more than once. One letter will not be used.)

R. $7.2 - n$ if $n = 6.5$

_____

T. $n + 4.31$ if $n = 2.9$

_____

H. $0.45 + n$ if $n = 1.7$

_____

S. $n - 3.8$ if $n = 4$

_____

L. $n + 3.1 - 2.6$ if $n = 1.4$

_____

I. $11 - n$ if $n = 6.43$

_____

C. $0.4 + n + 0.93$ if $n = 0.3$

_____

A. $n + 2 - 1.04$ if $n = 1.07$

_____

Y. $n - 3.1 - 0.02$ if $n = 6.4$

_____

O. $6.8 - 1.07 + n$ if $n = 2.5$

_____

M. $n - 4.301$ if $n = 5.2$

_____

N. $7.3 + n - 1.5$ if $n = 3$

_____

Hold on to Your Hat!

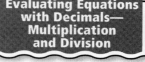

The highest point in the Northeast is in New Hampshire. This is also one of the windiest places on our planet. What is the name of this place?

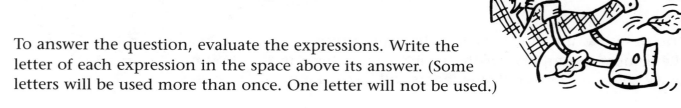

Answer:

$$\overline{\hspace{1em}}\ \overline{\hspace{1em}}\ \overline{\hspace{1em}}\ \overline{\hspace{1em}}\ \overline{\hspace{1em}}$$
0.3   2   1.792   3.7   56.32

$$\overline{\hspace{1em}}\ \overline{\hspace{1em}}\ \overline{\hspace{1em}}\ \overline{\hspace{1em}}\ \overline{\hspace{1em}}\ \overline{\hspace{1em}}\ \overline{\hspace{1em}}\ \overline{\hspace{1em}}\ \overline{\hspace{1em}}\ \overline{\hspace{1em}}$$
40   1.26   24.1   1.82   1.7   3.7   318.5   56.32   2   3.7

To answer the question, evaluate the expressions. Write the letter of each expression in the space above its answer. (Some letters will be used more than once. One letter will not be used.)

A. $n \times 1.4$ if $n = 0.9$

_____

H. $2.6 \times n$ if $n = 0.7$

_____

N. $7.4 \div n$ if $n = 2$

_____

I. $n \div 5$ if $n = 8.5$

_____

R. $n \times 0.04$ if $n = 84$

_____

S. $7.23 \div n$ if $n = 0.3$

_____

O. $n \div 4.5$ if $n = 9$

_____

U. $5.6 \times n$ if $n = 0.32$

_____

G. $n \times 4.9$ if $n = 65$

_____

M. $n \div 2.5$ if $n = 0.75$

_____

W. $6 \div n$ if $n = 0.15$

_____

T. $8.8 \times n$ if $n = 6.4$

_____

Practice, Practice, Practice! Algebra Readiness   Scholastic Teaching Resources

23

Exploring Underground

The deepest cave in the United States is part of an extensive system of caves in a southwestern state. What is the name of this system of caves?

Answer:

$\dfrac{}{4\frac{1}{2}}$ $\dfrac{}{7}$ $\dfrac{}{\frac{7}{9}}$ $\dfrac{}{\frac{3}{5}}$ $\dfrac{}{4}$ $\dfrac{}{\frac{1}{3}}$ $\dfrac{}{7}$ $\dfrac{}{1\frac{2}{3}}$

$\dfrac{}{4\frac{1}{2}}$ $\dfrac{}{7}$ $\dfrac{}{4\frac{4}{5}}$ $\dfrac{}{\frac{1}{2}}$ $\dfrac{}{\frac{7}{9}}$ $\dfrac{}{\frac{4}{5}}$ $\dfrac{}{4}$

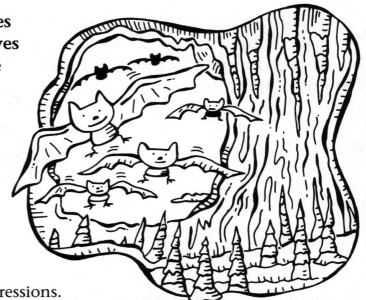

To answer the question, evaluate the expressions. (Remember to simplify.) Write the letter of each expression in the space above its answer. (Some letters will be used more than once.)

R. $\frac{2}{9} + n$ if $n = \frac{5}{9}$

_____

L. $\frac{4}{5} - n$ if $n = \frac{1}{5}$

_____

E. $\frac{3}{8} + n$ if $n = \frac{1}{8}$

_____

N. $n + \frac{7}{10}$ if $n = \frac{1}{10}$

_____

B. $\frac{11}{12} - n$ if $n = \frac{7}{12}$

_____

V. $4\frac{1}{10} + n$ if $n = \frac{7}{10}$

_____

S. $3\frac{2}{3} + n$ if $n = \frac{1}{3}$

_____

D. $n - 4\frac{1}{6}$ if $n = 5\frac{5}{6}$

_____

C. $7\frac{7}{8} - n$ if $n = 3\frac{3}{8}$

_____

A. $n + 1\frac{1}{2}$ if $n = 5\frac{1}{2}$

_____

Practice, Practice, Practice! Algebra Readiness   Scholastic Teaching Resources

Born on the Fourth of July

One American president was born on the Fourth of July. Who was he?

Answer:

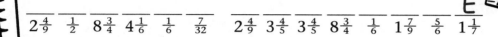

$$\overline{}\ \overline{}\ \overline{}\ \overline{}\ \overline{}\ \overline{}\quad \overline{}\ \overline{}\ \overline{}\ \overline{}\ \overline{}\ \overline{}\ \overline{}\ \overset{E}{\overline{}}$$

$$2\tfrac{4}{9}\quad \tfrac{1}{2}\quad 8\tfrac{3}{4}\quad 4\tfrac{1}{6}\quad \tfrac{1}{6}\quad \tfrac{7}{32}\qquad 2\tfrac{4}{9}\quad 3\tfrac{4}{5}\quad 3\tfrac{4}{5}\quad 8\tfrac{3}{4}\quad \tfrac{1}{6}\quad 1\tfrac{7}{9}\quad \tfrac{5}{6}\quad 1\tfrac{1}{7}$$

To answer the question above, evaluate each expression. (Remember to simplify.) Then write the corresponding letter on the line above its matching answer. (Some letters will be used more than once.) The first one has been done for you.

E. $n \div \tfrac{1}{2}$ if $n = \tfrac{4}{7}$

$$\underline{\qquad\qquad 1\tfrac{1}{7} \qquad\qquad}$$

G. $\tfrac{5}{8} \div n$ if $n = \tfrac{3}{4}$

_____

A. $n \times \tfrac{3}{5}$ if $n = \tfrac{5}{6}$

_____

N. $\tfrac{7}{12} \times n$ if $n = \tfrac{3}{8}$

_____

I. $\tfrac{3}{4} \times n$ if $n = \tfrac{2}{9}$

_____

L. $3\tfrac{1}{2} \times n$ if $n = 2\tfrac{1}{2}$

_____

D. $6\tfrac{2}{3} \div n$ if $n = 3\tfrac{3}{4}$

_____

V. $n \times 1\tfrac{1}{4}$ if $n = 3\tfrac{1}{3}$

_____

C. $n \div 1\tfrac{1}{2}$ if $n = 3\tfrac{2}{3}$

_____

O. $4\tfrac{3}{4} \div n$ if $n = 1\tfrac{1}{4}$

_____

Name _____ Date _____

Grab Your Umbrella

If you ever visit this place in Hawaii, be sure to bring your umbrella. It rains there about 350 days each year. What is the name of this very rainy place?

Answer:

$\overline{}$ $\overline{}$ $\overline{}$ $\overline{}$ $\overline{}$
22.24 73.6 6.72 12.3 57.87

$\overline{}$ $\overline{}$ $\overline{}$ $\overline{}$ $\overline{}$ $\overline{}$ $\overline{}$ $\overline{}$
45.78 1.82 18.9 1.82 9.3 4.45 1.82 9.3 4.45

To answer the question, solve the equations. Write the letter of the problem in the space above its answer. (Some letters will be used more than once. Some letters will not be used.)

I. $6.7 + n = 25.6$

_____

O. $n + 9.4 = 83$

_____

L. $n - 0.45 = 8.85$

_____

V. $n + 9.5 = 92.4$

_____

U. $7.3 + n = 14.02$

_____

M. $n - 14.9 = 7.34$

_____

E. $n - 0.85 = 3.6$

_____

S. $n - 2.8 = 1.8$

_____

W. $n - 45.6 = 0.18$

_____

N. $47.8 + n = 60.1$

_____

T. $n - 54.3 = 3.57$

_____

A. $n + 7.04 = 8.86$

_____

Practice, Practice, Practice! Algebra Readiness   Scholastic Teaching Resources

Turn on the Radio

In 1899, the first international radio signals were transmitted across the English Channel from England to France. Who was the man who transmitted these signals?

Answer:

$\overline{2.17}$ $\overline{71.3}$ $\overline{2.17}$ $\overline{3.6}$ $\overline{3.8}$ $\overline{5.22}$ $\overline{3.6}$ $\overline{0.004}$ $\overline{3}$ $\overline{}$

$\overline{0.004}$ $\overline{1.05}$ $\overline{0.28}$ $\overline{1.6}$ $\overline{3}$ $\overline{43.2}$ $\overline{3.8}$

To answer the question, solve the equations. Write the letter of the problem in the space above its answer. (Some letters will be used more than once. One letter will not be used.)

E. $n \div 6 = 0.87$

_____

A. $5 \times n = 5.25$

_____

N. $n \div 8 = 5.4$

_____

U. $n \div 23 = 3.1$

_____

R. $36 \times n = 10.08$

_____

H. $n \div 2.6 = 1.8$

_____

I. $n \times 0.04 = 0.152$

_____

G. $n \div 0.35 = 6.2$

_____

O. $n \div 0.05 = 60$

_____

L. $6.03 \times n = 21.708$

_____

M. $n \times 25 = 0.1$

_____

C. $n \div 0.25 = 6.4$

_____

Name _____ Date _____

It's a Gusher!

Oil is an important fuel. It is also an important part of products such as plastics, paints, building materials, and even clothing. The first successful oil well was drilled in the United States in 1859. Where was this well located?

Answer:

$$\overline{\quad} \ \overline{\quad} \ \overline{\quad} \ \overline{\quad} \ \overline{\quad} \ \overline{\quad} \ \overline{\quad} \ \overline{\quad} \ \overline{\quad} \ \overline{\quad} \ ,$$

15   $\frac{8}{11}$ 15 $\frac{1}{2}$ $\frac{1}{4}$ $1\frac{1}{4}$ $\frac{8}{11}$ $3\frac{7}{10}$ $3\frac{7}{10}$ $\frac{5}{9}$,

$4\frac{3}{5}$ $\frac{5}{9}$ $3\frac{1}{3}$ $3\frac{1}{3}$ $\frac{1}{4}$ $8\frac{3}{4}$ $3\frac{7}{10}$ $1\frac{1}{4}$ $\frac{14}{15}$ $3\frac{1}{3}$ $\frac{8}{11}$ $\frac{14}{15}$

To answer the question, solve the equations. (Remember to simplify.) Write the letter of the problem in the space above its answer. (Some letters will be used more than once. One letter will not be used.)

I. $n - \frac{3}{11} = \frac{5}{11}$

R. $n + 5\frac{3}{8} = 7$

E. $n + \frac{2}{9} = \frac{7}{9}$

L. $n - 2\frac{1}{2} = 1\frac{1}{5}$

S. $\frac{5}{8} + n = \frac{7}{8}$

T. $n - 6\frac{3}{7} = 8\frac{4}{7}$

U. $n - \frac{5}{12} = \frac{1}{12}$

Y. $n - 2\frac{1}{8} = 6\frac{5}{8}$

A. $n - \frac{3}{5} = \frac{1}{3}$

P. $7\frac{1}{3} + n = 11\frac{14}{15}$

V. $n + \frac{1}{8} = 1\frac{3}{8}$

N. $n + 4\frac{1}{6} = 7\frac{1}{2}$

28

Name _____ Date _____

Tarzan!

One of the best-known characters in English fiction is Tarzan, who was created in 1914. Since then, Tarzan has starred in stories, movies, and on TV. Who was the creator of Tarzan?

Answer:

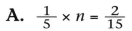

$$\overline{\rule{1cm}{0.4pt}}\ \overline{\rule{1cm}{0.4pt}}\ \overline{\rule{1cm}{0.4pt}}\ \overline{\rule{1cm}{0.4pt}}\ \overline{\rule{1cm}{0.4pt}}\qquad \overline{\rule{1cm}{0.4pt}}\ \overline{\rule{1cm}{0.4pt}}\ \overline{\rule{1cm}{0.4pt}}\ \overline{\rule{1cm}{0.4pt}}$$
$24\frac{1}{2}\quad 3\frac{1}{3}\quad \frac{3}{7}\quad \frac{2}{3}\quad 4\frac{3}{4}\qquad 4\frac{3}{4}\quad \frac{3}{4}\quad 2\frac{1}{2}\quad 24\frac{1}{2}$

$$\overline{\rule{1cm}{0.4pt}}\ \overline{\rule{1cm}{0.4pt}}\ \overline{\rule{1cm}{0.4pt}}\ \overline{\rule{1cm}{0.4pt}}\ \overline{\rule{1cm}{0.4pt}}\ \overline{\rule{1cm}{0.4pt}}\ \overline{\rule{1cm}{0.4pt}}\ \overline{\rule{1cm}{0.4pt}}\ \overline{\rule{1cm}{0.4pt}}$$
$5\frac{3}{5}\quad \frac{5}{8}\quad 4\frac{3}{4}\quad 4\frac{3}{4}\quad \frac{1}{10}\quad \frac{5}{8}\quad \frac{3}{7}\quad 9\quad 2$

To answer the question, solve the equations. (Remember to simplify.) Write the letter of the problem in the space above its answer. (Some letters will be used more than once.)

A. $\frac{1}{5} \times n = \frac{2}{15}$

_____

O. $n \div \frac{1}{5} = \frac{1}{2}$

_____

I. $n \div 3 = \frac{1}{4}$

_____

H. $n \times \frac{2}{3} = 6$

_____

U. $n \div \frac{3}{4} = \frac{5}{6}$

_____

G. $4\frac{2}{3} \times n = 2$

_____

S. $n \times 2\frac{3}{8} = 4\frac{3}{4}$

_____

D. $n \div \frac{5}{6} = 4$

_____

R. $n \div 1\frac{1}{4} = 3\frac{4}{5}$

_____

B. $n \div 4\frac{2}{3} = 1\frac{1}{5}$

_____

E. $n \div 2\frac{1}{3} = 10\frac{1}{2}$

_____

C. $3\frac{1}{2} \times n = 8\frac{3}{4}$

_____

Practice, Practice, Practice! Algebra Readiness   Scholastic Teaching Resources

29

Name _____   Date _____

Home, Sweet Home

Although our planet is big, all life exists in a relatively narrow band of land, sea, and sky. This part has the conditions life needs to survive. What is this part of Earth called?

Answer:

— — — — — — — — — — —

To answer the question, solve the inequalities. For each problem, four possible answers are given. Circle all answers that make each inequality true. When you are done, write the letters in order in the spaces.

1 $3 + n > 14$
- **R.** 4
- **B.** 12
- **T.** 10
- **I.** 13

4 $3n > 26$
- **D.** 8
- **M.** 7
- **K.** 3
- **H.** 9

2 $n - 6 < 3$
- **H.** 9
- **E.** 10
- **O.** 8
- **U.** 12

5 $2n \div 4 > 3$
- **E.** 10
- **L.** 6
- **T.** 2
- **R.** 8

3 $n \div 4 > 6$
- **S.** 28
- **E.** 24
- **C.** 20
- **P.** 32

6 $4(n + 5) < 33$
- **H.** 4
- **S.** 5
- **E.** 3
- **I.** 6

30

Time for Reading

The first library for children in the United States opened in Connecticut in 1803. In what town was this library located?

Answer:

___ ___ ___ ___ ___ ___ ___ ___ ___
1   2   3   4   5   6   7   8   9

To answer the question, solve the inequalities. For each problem, four possible answers are given. Circle the answer that makes the inequality true, then write the letter of each answer in the space above its problem number.

1 $n + 2.1 > 3.5$
- **R.** 0.857
- **B.** 1.34
- **S.** 1.5
- **C.** 0.2

2 $n - 0.35 < 7.04$
- **E.** 27.4
- **A.** 7.19
- **I.** 7.635
- **T.** 12

3 $4n > 12.25$
- **J.** 2.96
- **M.** 0.4
- **T.** 0.254
- **L.** 3.3

4 $n \div 2 < 0.32$
- **R.** 1.6
- **G.** 4
- **J.** 0.8
- **I.** 0.6202

5 $n - 0.38 < 1.01$
- **W.** 2.0
- **R.** 1.9
- **S.** 1.2
- **K.** 3

6 $2.75n < 8.25$
- **B.** 2.9
- **E.** 3.05
- **L.** 3
- **H.** 4.1

7 $14.05 + n > 15$
- **M.** 0.364
- **U.** 0.96
- **V.** 0.906
- **J.** 0.205

8 $n \div 6 > 0.38$
- **D.** 1.26
- **A.** 0.96
- **K.** 1.6
- **R.** 2.4

9 $n + 0.03 > 1.037$
- **S.** 0.304
- **W.** 1.0038
- **E.** 1.0065
- **Y.** 1.008

Name _____ Date _____

Alive and Well

Your body is composed of individual cells all working together to keep you alive and help you to grow. About how many cells make up the human body?

Answer:

‾1‾ ‾2‾ ‾3‾ ‾4‾ ‾5‾ ‾6‾ ‾7‾ ‾8‾ ‾9‾ ‾10‾ ‾11‾ ‾12‾ ‾13‾

To answer the question, solve each proportion. Find your answers in the Answer Box, then write the letter of each answer in the space above its problem number. (Some letters will be used more than once. Some letters will not be used.)

1 $\frac{2}{5} = \frac{n}{20}$

$n =$ _____

5 $\frac{n}{5} = \frac{24}{10}$

$n =$ _____

9 $\frac{n}{36} = \frac{1}{4}$

$n =$ _____

13 $\frac{20}{n} = \frac{4}{3}$

$n =$ _____

2 $\frac{3}{n} = \frac{9}{30}$

$n =$ _____

6 $\frac{3}{27} = \frac{9}{n}$

$n =$ _____

10 $\frac{6}{22} = \frac{n}{33}$

$n =$ _____

3 $\frac{n}{16} = \frac{4}{8}$

$n =$ _____

7 $\frac{5}{12} = \frac{n}{60}$

$n =$ _____

11 $\frac{40}{25} = \frac{16}{n}$

$n =$ _____

4 $\frac{9}{n} = \frac{1}{9}$

$n =$ _____

8 $\frac{6}{15} = \frac{4}{n}$

$n =$ _____

12 $\frac{10}{15} = \frac{n}{30}$

$n =$ _____

Answer Box

Y. 12

I. 10

L. 9

B. 18

F. 8

M. 36

O. 20

N. 15

T. 81

R. 25

Practice, Practice, Practice! Algebra Readiness Scholastic Teaching Resources

Big Water

The largest body of fresh water that lies entirely in the United States is 306 miles long and 118 miles wide. What is the name of this body of water?

Answer:

___ ___ ___ ___   ___ ___ ___ ___ ___ ___ ___ ___
 1   2   3   4   5   6   7   8   9   10 11 12

To answer the question, solve each proportion. Find your answers in the Answer Box, then write the letter of each answer in the space above its problem number. (Some letters will be used more than once. Some letters will not be used.)

1 $\dfrac{3}{5} = \dfrac{n}{15}$

n = _____

5 $\dfrac{21}{12} = \dfrac{n}{28}$

n = _____

9 $\dfrac{n}{36} = \dfrac{10}{15}$

n = _____

2 $\dfrac{4}{n} = \dfrac{8}{32}$

n = _____

6 $\dfrac{9}{12} = \dfrac{n}{32}$

n = _____

10 $\dfrac{3.5}{7} = \dfrac{n}{6}$

n = _____

3 $\dfrac{1.4}{2.1} = \dfrac{8}{n}$

n = _____

7 $\dfrac{21}{n} = \dfrac{2.6}{7.8}$

n = _____

11 $\dfrac{7}{4} = \dfrac{28}{n}$

n = _____

4 $\dfrac{9}{n} = \dfrac{1.5}{3.5}$

n = _____

8 $\dfrac{n}{25} = \dfrac{3}{5}$

n = _____

12 $\dfrac{2.5}{n} = \dfrac{3}{6}$

n = _____

Answer Box

K. 12
H. 15
I. 24
M. 49
L. 9
S. 10
N. 5
U. 25
C. 63
G. 3
A. 16
E. 21

Name _____ Date _____

A Wonderful Land

Most people are familiar with the story *Alice's Adventures in Wonderland,* written by Lewis Carroll. Many do not realize that Lewis Carroll was not the author's real name. What was his real name?

Answer:

___ ___ ___ ___ ___ ___ ___
104 150   8 20.16 40   52 26.25

___ ___ ___ ___ ___ ___ ___ ___   ___ ___ ___ ___ ___ ___ ___
40   54 107.8 78   105 72   9   52   72 4.16 72   9 26.25 4.16 62.64

To answer the question, find the percent of each number.
Write the letter of the problem in the space above its answer.
(Some letters will be used more than once.)

L. 50% of 80 = n

$n = $ _____

D. 75% of 96 = n

$n = $ _____

T. 110% of 98 = n

$n = $ _____

W. 65% of 120 = n

$n = $ _____

O. 8% of 52 = n

$n = $ _____

S. 35% of 75 = n

$n = $ _____

G. 25% of 36 = n

$n = $ _____

E. 80% of 65 = n

$n = $ _____

C. 130% of 80 = n

$n = $ _____

U. 36% of 150 = n

$n = $ _____

I. 125% of 84 = n

$n = $ _____

N. 54% of 116 = n

$n = $ _____

A. 5% of 160 = n

$n = $ _____

R. 28% of 72 = n

$n = $ _____

H. 150% of 100 = n

$n = $ _____

Practice, Practice, Practice! Algebra Readiness Scholastic Teaching Resources

Name _____ Date _____

A Presidential Mathematician

An American president wrote and published an original proof of the Pythagorean Theorem. Who was this president?

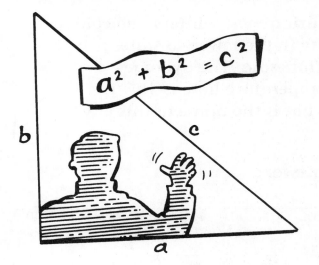

$$a^2 + b^2 = c^2$$

Answer:

___ ___ ___ ___ ___
50.44 88.74 57.8 18.24 66

___ ___ ___ ___ ___ ___ ___ ___
4.75 88.74 8.91 62.5 36.32 18.24 222.6 3.54

To answer the question, find the percent of each number. Write the letter of the problem in the space above its answer. (Some letters will be used more than once. One letter will not be used.)

E. 24% of 76 = n

$n =$ _____

D. 3% of 118 = n

$n =$ _____

A. 87% of 102 = n

$n =$ _____

I. $56\frac{3}{4}$% of 64 = n

$n =$ _____

L. 105% of 212 = n

$n =$ _____

J. 48.5% of 104 = n

$n =$ _____

R. 16.5% of 54 = n

$n =$ _____

F. 125% of 50 = n

$n =$ _____

U. $23\frac{1}{4}$% of 96 = n

$n =$ _____

G. 12.5% of 38 = n

$n =$ _____

S. 75% of 88 = n

$n =$ _____

M. $72\frac{1}{4}$% of 80 = n

$n =$ _____

Practice, Practice, Practice! Algebra Readiness   Scholastic Teaching Resources

35

Name _____ Date _____

Turn Up the Heat

During most winters, the coldest city in the lower 48 states is in Minnesota. The average temperature here is 36.8°F. What is the name of this city?

Answer:

———
25% 20% 40% 15% 50% 20% 200% 40% 25% 120% 20% 200% 60%

——————————————————————————————
12% 200% 60% 60% 100%

To answer the question, find each percent. Write the letter of each problem in the space above its answer. (Some letters will be used more than once. Some letters will not be used.)

E. $n\%$ of $520 = 78$

$n =$ _____

S. $10 = n\%$ of 10

$n =$ _____

L. $48 = n\%$ of 80

$n =$ _____

O. $n\%$ of $50 = 60$

$n =$ _____

R. $12 = n\%$ of 24

$n =$ _____

B. $12 = n\%$ of 40

$n =$ _____

U. $12 = n\%$ of 50

$n =$ _____

N. $n\%$ of $30 = 6$

$n =$ _____

I. $n\%$ of $28 = 7$

$n =$ _____

A. $n\%$ of $24 = 48$

$n =$ _____

F. $60 = n\%$ of 500

$n =$ _____

T. $28 = n\%$ of 70

$n =$ _____

Practice, Practice, Practice! Algebra Readiness Scholastic Teaching Resources

Name _____ Date _____

A First

The first four-function, mechanical calculator was built in the late 1600s. Who was its inventor?

Answer:

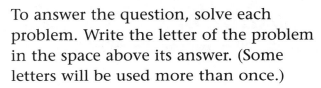

$\overline{}$ $\overline{}$ $\overline{}$ $\overline{}$ $\overline{}$ $\overline{}$ $\overline{}$ $\overline{}$ $\overline{}$
80 160 200 200 60 125 55 30 84

$\overline{}$ $\overline{}$ $\overline{}$ $\overline{}$ $\overline{}$ $\overline{}$ $\overline{}$
100 30 55 400 40 55 21

To answer the question, solve each problem. Write the letter of the problem in the space above its answer. (Some letters will be used more than once.)

L. 14% of n = 14

_____

F. 50% of n = 30

_____

E. 12 = 40% of n

_____

Z. 42 = 200% of n

_____

O. 15% of n = 24

_____

N. 15% of n = 6

_____

R. 60 = 48% of n

_____

D. 75% of n = 63

_____

G. 125% of n = 100

_____

I. 80% of n = 44

_____

T. 11% of n = 22

_____

B. 3% of n = 12

_____

Name _____ Date _____

Food for Thought

When Thomas Jefferson returned from France, where he served as a U.S. ambassador, he introduced a new food to our country. What was the name of this food?

Answer:

$\overline{}$ $\overline{}$ $\overline{}$ $\overline{}$ $\overline{}$ $\overline{}$ $\overline{}$ $\overline{}$
60% 160% 800 135 9 30 9 68%

To answer the question, solve each problem. Write the letter of the problem in the space above its answer. Then rewrite the letters from right to left. (One letter will be used twice. Some letters will not be used.)

R. 150% of 90 = n

_____

T. 21 = 30% of n

_____

C. 30% of n = 9

_____

I. 18 = n% of 30

_____

N. n% of 25 = 40

_____

O. 25% of n = 200

_____

S. 50% of n = 12

_____

M. 17 = n% of 25

_____

A. 20% of 45 = n

_____

Practice, Practice, Practice! Algebra Readiness   Scholastic Teaching Resources

Name _____   Date _____

Chips

Potato chips were invented in 1853, but they were not called potato chips. They were named partly after the place in New York where they were first created. What were potato chips originally called?

Answer:

___ ___ ___ ___ ___ ___ ___ ___ Chips
$3 25% 10 25% $15 30% 24% 25%

To answer the question, first find the increase or decrease, then the percent of increase or decrease for each item. Write the letter of each answer in the space above the answer. (One letter will be used more than once. Some letters will not be used.)

Item	Previous Price or Average	Current Price or Average	Increase or Decrease	% of Increase or Decrease
CD	$12	$15	___ S	___ A
Hourly Wage	$5	$7	___ M	___ N
Math Average	80	70	___ R	___ B
Sneakers	$50	$35	___ T	___ O
Bowling Average	125	120	___ L	___ D
Annual Dues	$50	$38	___ I	___ G

Practice, Practice, Practice! Algebra Readiness Scholastic Teaching Resources

39

Name _____ Date _____

The Powers of Exponents

The largest freshwater fish in the world is found in Asia. It can grow to be 10 feet long and weigh as much as 1,600 pounds. What is the name of this fish?

Answer:

$\overline{}$ $\overline{}$ $\overline{}$ $\overline{}$ $\overline{}$ $\overline{}$ $\overline{}$
32 16 100 81 343 144 343

$\overline{}$ $\overline{}$ $\overline{}$ $\overline{}$ $\overline{}$ $\overline{}$ $\overline{}$ $\overline{}$ $\overline{}$ $\overline{}$
64 0 243 243 125 343 36 100 144 16

To answer the question, find the value of each expression. Write the letter of the problem in the space above its answer. (Some letters will be used more than once. Some letters will not be used.)

H. $2^4 = $ _____

N. $9^2 = $ _____

E. $7^3 = $ _____

G. $3^3 = $ _____

L. $5^3 = $ _____

M. $2^8 = $ _____

Y. $2^3 = $ _____

D. $3^5 = $ _____

P. $4^3 = $ _____

I. $10^2 = $ _____

F. $6^2 = $ _____

C. $2^5 = $ _____

S. $12^2 = $ _____

A. $0^5 = $ _____

O. $3^6 = $ _____

Name _____ Date _____

The Official White House

The White House is the home of the President of the United States. It was not always called the White House. In the past it has been called the Presidential Palace, the President's House, and the Executive Mansion. Which president gave the White House its official name?

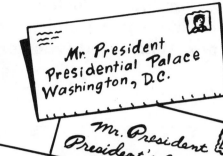

Answer:

$\overline{85}$ $\overline{9}$ $\overline{103}$ $\overline{4}$ $\overline{17}$ $\overline{4}$ $\overline{50}$ $\overline{103}$

$\overline{50}$ $\overline{4}$ $\overline{4}$ $\overline{21}$ $\overline{103}$ $\overline{6}$ $\overline{103}$ $\overline{26}$ $\overline{85}$

To answer the question, simplify the expressions. Write the letter of each expression in the space above its answer. (Some letters will be used more than once. Some letters will not be used.)

L. $2(3^2 + 4) =$ _____

R. $(4 + 8^2) - 2(4^2 - 7) =$ _____

D. $8 + (6^2 \div 4) =$ _____

T. $6(7^2 - 6^2) + (9 - 2) =$ _____

E. $9(3 + 2^3) + 4 =$ _____

U. $(3 \times 2)^2 - (6 - 4)^2 =$ _____

H. $2(4 + 8) - (5^2 - 10) =$ _____

V. $18 \div 3^2 + (9 - 7)^2 =$ _____

S. $3^3 - (4^2 - 10) =$ _____

W. $(7 + 3^2)(16 - 4^2) =$ _____

M. $(16 \div 2^2) + (5^2 - 14) =$ _____

O. $8(3^1 + 5) \div (1 + 3)^2 =$ _____

The First Vaccine

In 1796, an English doctor developed the first vaccine. This vaccine prevented smallpox. Who was this doctor?

Answer:

$$\overline{}\ \overline{}\ \overline{}\ \overline{}\ \overline{}\ \overline{}\quad \overline{}\ \overline{}\ \overline{}\ \overline{}\ \overline{}\ \overline{}$$
1 2 3 4 5 6   7 8 9 10 11 12

To answer the question, write >, <, or = to make each equation or inequality true. Write the letter beneath the sign in the space above the problem number.

1 $5 + 3$ ____ 3^2

    >   <   =
    T   E   M

2 $4^2 + 10$ ____ $2(7 + 5)$

    >   <   =
    D   H   B

3 9^3 ____ $9(8 + 9)$

    >   <   =
    W   O   Y

4 $130 - 5$ ____ $5^3 - 1$

    >   <   =
    A   K   M

5 $(18 + 2^2) + 8$ ____ 62

    >   <   =
    S   R   A

6 $(5^2 + 3) \div 7$ ____ $(3 - 1)^2$

    >   <   =
    U   V   D

7 $24 - (8 - 4)^2$ ____ $6^2 \div 4$

    >   <   =
    R   J   U

8 $36 \div (2^2 + 2)$ ____ 2×3

    >   <   =
    N   J   E

9 $2^6 - 2$ ____ $8^2 - 6$

    >   <   =
    N   D   C

10 $5(9 - 3^2)$ ____ 37

    >   <   =
    R   N   L

11 12^2 ____ $2 \times 2^3 \times 9$

    >   <   =
    I   F   E

12 $(5 - 3)^3 (8 - 3)^2$ ____ $10^2 + 30$

    >   <   =
    R   A   K

Practice, Practice, Practice! Algebra Readiness   Scholastic Teaching Resources

A Ride in Space

On June 18, 1983, this astronaut became the first U.S. woman to travel in space. What is her name?

Answer:

$\dfrac{}{1}$ $\dfrac{}{2}$ $\dfrac{}{3}$ $\dfrac{}{4}$ $\dfrac{}{5}$ $\dfrac{}{6}$. $\dfrac{}{7}$ $\dfrac{}{8}$ $\dfrac{}{9}$ $\dfrac{}{10}$

To answer the question, find the square root of each number. Round answers to the nearest tenth if necessary. Find your answers in the Answer Box, then write the letter of each answer in the space above the problem number. (One letter will be used more than once. Some letters will not be used.)

Answer Box
K. 1.4
A. 5
N. 25
L. 8.4
R. 7.5
S. 7
I. 1
T. 12.5
Y. 4.9
D. 7.1
E. 3
U. 28

1 $\sqrt{49}$ = _____

2 $\sqrt{25}$ = _____

3 $\sqrt{70}$ = _____

4 $\sqrt{71}$ = _____

5 $\sqrt{24}$ = _____

6 $\sqrt{2}$ = _____

7 $\sqrt{56}$ = _____

8 $\sqrt{1}$ = _____

9 $\sqrt{50}$ = _____

10 $\sqrt{9}$ = _____

Practice, Practice, Practice! Algebra Readiness   Scholastic Teaching Resources

43

Name _____ Date _____

Roll the Presses

The first printing press in the American colonies was set up in 1639. In what state was this press located?

Answer:

$\overline{}$ $\overline{}$ $\overline{}$ $\overline{}$ $\overline{}$ $\overline{}$ $\overline{}$ $\overline{}$ $\overline{}$ $\overline{}$ $\overline{}$ $\overline{}$ $\overline{}$
135 25   75   75   25 100 400 300   75   90 225 225   75

To answer the question, use the figure to find the areas of the squares and rectangles. Write the letter of each problem in the space above its answer. (Some letters will be used more than once.)

Use these formulas: Area of a square = s^2

Area of a rectangle = $l \times w$

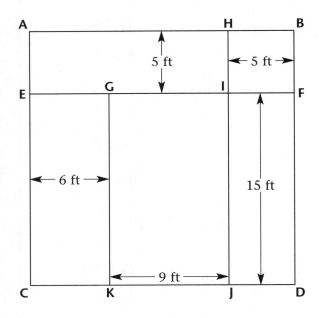

H. Area of square *ABDC* = _____ sq ft

E. Area of rectangle *EGKC* = _____ sq ft

A. Area of square *HBFI* = _____ sq ft

U. Area of rectangle *EFDC* = _____ sq ft

T. Area of square *EIJC* = _____ sq ft

M. Area of rectangle *GIJK* = _____ sq ft

C. Area of rectangle *HBDJ* = _____ sq ft

S. Area of rectangle *IFDJ* = _____ sq ft

Practice, Practice, Practice! Algebra Readiness Scholastic Teaching Resources

The Biggest Sleepyhead

Averaging about 22 hours of sleep each day, this animal is considered to be the sleepiest of all animals. What is this sleepy animal?

Answer: $\overline{}\ \overline{}\ \overline{}\ \overline{}\ \overline{}$
          88 160   88   144   48

To answer the question, find the area of each triangle. Write the letter of the triangle in the space above its area. When you are done, reverse the letters. (One letter will be used more than once. Some letters will not be used.)

Use this formula: Area of a triangle = $\frac{1}{2}bh$

S.

b = 10 ft
h = 12 ft

A = _____ sq ft

R.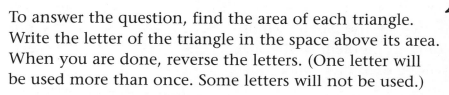

b = 2 ft
h = 12 ft

A = _____ sq ft

K.

b = 16 ft
h = 6 ft

A = _____ sq ft

O.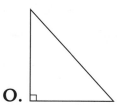

b = 16 ft
h = 18 ft

A = _____ sq ft

L.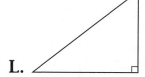

b = 20 ft
h = 16 ft

A = _____ sq ft

A.

b = 8 ft
h = 22 ft

A = _____ sq ft

J.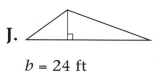

b = 24 ft
h = 6 ft

A = _____ sq ft

T.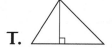

b = 14 ft
h = 9 ft

A = _____ sq ft

E.

b = 16 ft
h = 7 ft

A = _____ sq ft

Name _____   Date _____

Pick a Book of Your Choice

With more than 23,000,000 books, this
U.S. library is the largest in the world.
What is the name of this library?

Answer:

Library ___ ___   ___ ___ ___ ___ ___ ___ ___ ___
      88 96   76 88 121 72 48 64 216 216

To answer the question, find the areas of the parallelograms
and trapezoids. Write the letter of each problem in the space
above its answer. (Some letters will be used more than once.)

Use these formulas: Area of a parallelogram = bh

Area of a trapezoid = $\frac{1}{2}(b_1 + b_2)h$

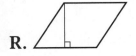

R.

$b = 8$ ft
$h = 6$ ft

$A =$ _____ sq ft

O.

$b_1 = 12$ ft
$b_2 = 10$ ft
$h = 8$ ft

$A =$ _____ sq ft

F.

$b = 16$ ft
$h = 6$ ft

$A =$ _____ sq ft

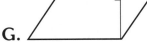

G.

$b = 12$ ft
$h = 6$ ft

$A =$ _____ sq ft

E.

$b_1 = 6$ ft
$b_2 = 10$ ft
$h = 8$ ft

$A =$ _____ sq ft

C.

$b_1 = 16$ ft
$b_2 = 22$ ft
$h = 4$ ft

$A =$ _____ sq ft

N.

$b_1 = 10$ ft
$b_2 = 12$ ft
$h = 11$ ft

$A =$ _____ sq ft

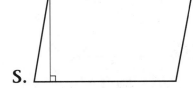

S.

$b = 18$ ft
$h = 12$ ft

$A =$ _____ sq ft

Practice, Practice, Practice! Algebra Readiness   Scholastic Teaching Resources

Name _____ Date _____

Sky Gazing

With a diameter of 640 miles, Ceres is the largest one of these in our solar system. What is Ceres?

Answer: _____
615.44 200.96 25.12 78.5 37.68 62.8 31.4 87.92

To answer the question, find the area and circumference of each circle. Use 3.14 for π. Write the letter of each area and circumference in the space above its answer. (Some letters will not be used.)

Use these formulas: Area of a circle = πr^2

Circumference of a circle = πd

1 (circle, $d = 8$)

   U. Area = _____ sq units

   T. Circumference = _____ units

2 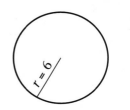 (circle, $r = 6$)

   M. Area = _____ sq units

   R. Circumference = _____ units

3 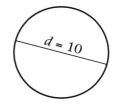 (circle, $d = 10$)

   E. Area = _____ sq units

   I. Circumference = _____ units

4 (circle, $d = 16$)

   S. Area = _____ sq units

   K. Circumference = _____ units

5 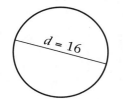 (circle, $r = 10$)

   L. Area = _____ sq units

   O. Circumference = _____ units

6  (circle, $r = 14$)

   A. Area = _____ sq units

   D. Circumference = _____ units

Practice, Practice, Practice! Algebra Readiness Scholastic Teaching Resources

Name _____   Date _____

What's in the Fridge?

In 1851, the first patent for mechanical refrigeration was awarded to an American inventor. The basic process this man invented is still used today. What was his name?

Answer:

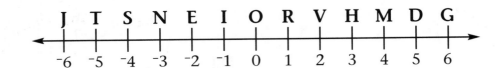

‾‾ ‾‾ ‾‾ ‾‾ ‾‾ ‾‾ ‾‾ ‾‾ ‾‾ ‾‾
 1   2   3   4   5   6   7   8   9   10

To answer the question, find the point described in each problem on the number line and write it on the space provided next to each problem. Write the letter of the point in the space above its problem number. (Some of the letters will be used more than once. Some letters will not be used.)

```
     J   T   S   N   E   I   O   R   V   H   M   D   G
 ←---+---+---+---+---+---+---+---+---+---+---+---+---+--→
    ‾6  ‾5  ‾4  ‾3  ‾2  ‾1   0   1   2   3   4   5   6
```

1 It is the smallest number that is pictured on the graph. _____

2 It is halfway between ‾1 and ⁺1. _____

3 It is 3 units to the right of 0. _____

4 It is 3 units to the right of ‾6. _____

5 It is the largest number that is graphed. _____

6 It is neither positive nor negative. _____

7 It is 4 units to the right of ‾3. _____

8 It is 5 units to the left of ⁺6. _____

9 It is 4 units to the left of ⁺3. _____

10 It is halfway between ‾3 and ‾1. _____

48

Practice, Practice, Practice! Algebra Readiness   Scholastic Teaching Resources

Name _____ Date _____

Fairy Tales

The Grimm Brothers collected and published fairy tales, including "Cinderella," "Rapunzel," and "Rumpelstiltskin." What were the full names of the Grimm Brothers?

Answer:

$\overline{54}$ $\overline{5}$ $\overline{3}$ $\overline{7}$ $\overline{0}$ $\overline{24}$ $\overline{15}$ $\overline{6}$ $\overline{53}$ $\overline{17}$ $\overline{62}$ $\overline{2}$ $\overline{5}$ $\overline{23}$ $\overline{24}$

and $\overline{53}$ $\overline{17}$ $\overline{24}$ $\overline{9}$ $\overline{8}$ $\overline{24}$ $\overline{12}$ $\overline{2}$ $\overline{5}$ $\overline{23}$ $\overline{24}$

To answer the question, write the absolute value of the numbers and complete the number sentences below. Write the letter of each problem in the space above its answer. (Some letters will be used more than once. Some letters will not be used.)

D. $|{}^+6| =$ _____

E. $|{}^-8| =$ _____

I. $|{}^+17| =$ _____

C. $|{}^+3| =$ _____

P. $|{}^-14| =$ _____

M. $|{}^-12| =$ _____

B. $|0| =$ _____

A. $|{}^-5| =$ _____

H. $|{}^+9| =$ _____

S. $|{}^-16| =$ _____

R. $|{}^+23| =$ _____

U. $|{}^-15| =$ _____

O. $|{}^+14| - |{}^-7| =$ _____

K. $|{}^-19| - |{}^+17| =$ _____

G. $|{}^+52| + |{}^-10| =$ _____

W. $|{}^+44| + |{}^-9| =$ _____

L. $|{}^-18| + |6| =$ _____

J. $|{}^-64| - |10| =$ _____

Name _____ Date _____

Big Wings

With a wingspan of nearly 10 feet, this seabird has the largest wingspan of any bird. What is the name of this bird?

Answer:

$\overline{\hspace{0.3em}14\hspace{0.3em}}$ $\overline{\hspace{0.3em}7\hspace{0.3em}}$ $\overline{\hspace{0.3em}8\hspace{0.3em}}$ $\overline{\hspace{0.3em}3\hspace{0.3em}}$ $\overline{\hspace{0.3em}18\hspace{0.3em}}$ $\overline{\hspace{0.3em}10\hspace{0.3em}}$ $\overline{\hspace{0.3em}12\hspace{0.3em}}$ $\overline{\hspace{0.3em}4\hspace{0.3em}}$ $\overline{\hspace{0.3em}13\hspace{0.3em}}$

$\overline{\hspace{0.3em}15\hspace{0.3em}}$ $\overline{\hspace{0.3em}9\hspace{0.3em}}$ $\overline{\hspace{0.3em}16\hspace{0.3em}}$ $\overline{\hspace{0.3em}6\hspace{0.3em}}$ $\overline{\hspace{0.3em}1\hspace{0.3em}}$ $\overline{\hspace{0.3em}11\hspace{0.3em}}$ $\overline{\hspace{0.3em}2\hspace{0.3em}}$ $\overline{\hspace{0.3em}5\hspace{0.3em}}$ $\overline{\hspace{0.3em}17\hspace{0.3em}}$

To answer the question, use > or < to make each number sentence true. Write the letter beneath the sign in the space above the problem number.

1 $^-8$ ____ $^+7$
   >   <
   K   T

2 $^-3$ ____ $^+8$
   >   <
   S   O

3 4 ____ $^-7$
   >   <
   D   L

4 $^-2$ ____ $^+5$
   >   <
   R   N

5 0 ____ $^-2$
   >   <
   S   G

6 $^+11$ ____ $^-12$
   >   <
   A   W

7 $^-2$ ____ 0
   >   <
   V   A

8 $^+8$ ____ $^+5$
   >   <
   N   P

9 $^+5$ ____ $^-6$
   >   <
   L   U

10 11 ____ $^-15$
   >   <
   R   C

11 $^-1$ ____ 0
   >   <
   O   R

12 $^-8$ ____ $^+4$
   >   <
   L   I

13 $^-6$ ____ $^-5$
   >   <
   S   G

14 $^-2$ ____ $^+2$
   >   <
   C   W

15 0 ____ $^-3$
   >   <
   A   N

16 $^+3$ ____ $^-8$
   >   <
   B   H

17 $^-7$ ____ $^+2$
   >   <
   M   S

18 2 ____ $^-6$
   >   <
   E   A

Play Ball

The first World Series was played in 1903.
One of the teams was the Pittsburgh Pirates.
What was the name of the other team?

Answer:

$\dfrac{}{1} \quad \dfrac{}{2} \quad \dfrac{}{3} \quad \dfrac{}{4} \quad \dfrac{}{5} \quad \dfrac{}{6}$

$\dfrac{}{7} \quad \dfrac{}{8} \quad \dfrac{}{9} \quad \dfrac{}{10} \quad \dfrac{}{11} \quad \dfrac{}{12} \quad \dfrac{}{13} \quad \dfrac{}{14}$

To answer the question, solve each problem. Find your answers in the Answer Box, then write the letter of each answer in the space above its problem number. (Some letters will be used more than once.)

1 $^-2 + {}^-3 =$ _____

2 $^-9 + {}^+9 =$ _____

3 $^-9 + {}^-7 =$ _____

4 $0 + {}^-9 =$ _____

5 $^+3 + {}^-3 =$ _____

6 $^+14 + {}^-11 =$ _____

7 $^-10 + {}^-3 =$ _____

8 $^-82 + {}^+68 =$ _____

9 $^-5 + {}^+20 =$ _____

10 $^+3 + {}^-9 =$ _____

11 $^-8 + {}^+7 + {}^+5 =$ _____

12 $^-8 + {}^-8 + {}^+2 =$ _____

13 $^-56 + {}^+24 =$ _____

14 $^-89 + {}^+73 =$ _____

Answer Box	
T.	$^-9$
O.	0
P.	$^-13$
G.	$^-6$
I.	$^-14$
B.	$^-5$
S.	$^-16$
L.	$^+15$
R.	$^+4$
N.	$^+3$
M.	$^-32$

Practice, Practice, Practice! Algebra Readiness   Scholastic Teaching Resources

51

Name _____ Date _____

Top of the Morning

The place where the morning sun first shines on the U.S. mainland is in Maine. What is the name of this place?

Answer:

$\overline{\rule{0.5cm}{0pt}}$ $\overline{\rule{0.5cm}{0pt}}$ $\overline{\rule{0.5cm}{0pt}}$ $\overline{\rule{0.5cm}{0pt}}$ $\overline{\rule{0.5cm}{0pt}}$ $\overline{\rule{0.5cm}{0pt}}$ $\overline{\rule{0.5cm}{0pt}}$ $\overline{\rule{0.5cm}{0pt}}$ $\overline{\rule{0.5cm}{0pt}}$ $\overline{\rule{0.5cm}{0pt}}$ $\overline{\rule{0.5cm}{0pt}}$ $\overline{\rule{0.5cm}{0pt}}$ $\overline{\rule{0.5cm}{0pt}}$
  1   2   3   4   5   6   7   8   9   10   11   12   13

To answer the question, solve each problem. Find your answers in the Answer Box, then write the letter of each answer in the space above its problem number. (Some letters will be used more than once.)

1 $^-2 - {}^+3 = $ _____

2 $^-8 - {}^-8 = $ _____

3 $^-14 - {}^+2 = $ _____

4 $^-6 - {}^-8 = $ _____

5 $^-12 - {}^+8 = $ _____

6 $^-33 - {}^-18 = $ _____

7 $^+12 - {}^-4 = $ _____

8 $^-10 - {}^+10 = $ _____

9 $^+8 - {}^-8 = $ _____

10 $^-17 - {}^+4 = $ _____

11 $^+27 - {}^+30 = $ _____

12 $^-15 - {}^+8 = $ _____

13 $^+9 - {}^+7 = $ _____

Answer Box
A. $^+16$
O. 0
N. $^+2$
T. $^-20$
H. $^-21$
I. $^-23$
M. $^-5$
U. $^-16$
K. $^-15$
D. $^-3$

The First Video Game

The first home video game system was produced in 1972. It was black and white and had only one game. What company manufactured this game, and what was the game called?

Answer:

$$\overline{\ \ 3\ \ }\ \overline{\ 14\ }\ \overline{\ 15\ }\ \overline{\ \ 1\ \ }\ \overline{\ \ 4\ \ }\ \overline{\ 10\ }\ \overline{\ \ 5\ \ }\ \overline{\ 11\ }\ ,$$

$$\overline{\ \ 2\ \ }\ \overline{\ \ 8\ \ }\ \overline{\ \ 9\ \ }\ \overline{\ \ 6\ \ }\ \overline{\ 12\ }\ \overline{\ \ 7\ \ }\ \overline{\ 13\ }$$

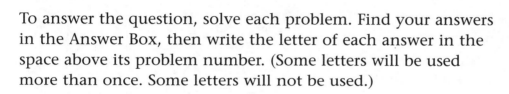

To answer the question, solve each problem. Find your answers in the Answer Box, then write the letter of each answer in the space above its problem number. (Some letters will be used more than once. Some letters will not be used.)

1 $^-4 \times {}^-7 = $ _____

2 $^-3 \times {}^+4 = $ _____

3 $^+3 \times {}^+9 = $ _____

4 $^-3 \times {}^+5 = $ _____

5 $^-24 \div {}^+2 = $ _____

6 $^+20 \div {}^-5 = $ _____

7 $^+27 \times {}^+3 = $ _____

8 $^-51 \div {}^-3 = $ _____

9 $^+36 \div {}^-2 = $ _____

10 $^-20 \times {}^-2 = $ _____

11 $^-81 \div {}^+9 = $ _____

12 $^-2 \times {}^+2 = $ _____

13 $^+6 \times {}^-3 = $ _____

14 $^+45 \div {}^-3 = $ _____

15 $^-90 \div {}^-9 = $ _____

Answer Box
A. $^-15$
V. $^+40$
R. $^+36$
O. $^-12$
G. $^+10$
D. $^+17$
X. $^-9$
Y. $^-18$
M. $^+27$
N. $^+28$
T. $^+6$
S. $^-4$
E. $^+81$

Name _____ Date _____

A Presidential Pet

Several presidents have had somewhat unusual pets in the White House. One of President Benjamin Harrison's pets pulled his grandchildren around in a cart. What type of pet was this, and what was its name?

Answer: $\overline{}_{12}\ \overline{}_{4}\ \overline{}_{8}\ \overline{}_{1}$,

$\overline{}_{9}\ \overline{}_{14}\ \overline{}_{15}\ \ \overline{}_{2}\ \overline{}_{13}\ \overline{}_{11}\ \overline{}_{5}\ \overline{}_{3}\ \overline{}_{6}\ \overline{}_{10}\ \overline{}_{7}$

To answer the question, solve each problem. Find your answers in the Answer Box, then write the letter of each answer in the space above its problem number. (Some letters will be used more than once.)

1 $^-7 - {}^+9 =$ _____

2 $^-20 + {}^-2 =$ _____

3 $^-8 + {}^+20 =$ _____

4 $^-8 \times 0 =$ _____

5 $^+8 - {}^+12 =$ _____

6 $^-9 \times {}^+2 =$ _____

7 $^+28 \div {}^-7 =$ _____

8 $^-4 \times {}^+5 =$ _____

9 $^-10 + {}^+10 =$ _____

10 $^+8 - {}^-3 =$ _____

11 $^-8 + {}^+6 =$ _____

12 $^-8 \times {}^-2 =$ _____

13 $^-12 + {}^+3 =$ _____

14 $^-36 \div {}^-2 =$ _____

15 $^-60 \div {}^-3 =$ _____

Answer Box

H. $^-9$
A. $^-20$
O. 0
W. $^-22$
G. $^+16$
I. $^-2$
L. $^+18$
K. $^+12$
T. $^-16$
E. $^-18$
D. $^+20$
S. $^-4$
R. $^+11$

Practice, Practice, Practice! Algebra Readiness Scholastic Teaching Resources

Name _____   Date _____

Model White House

A craftsman has spent over 40 years making a 60-foot by 20-foot model of the White House. What is the name of this man?

Answer: ———— ———— ———— ————
$^-9$ $^-18$ $^-4$ $^+5$

———— ———— ———— ———— ———— ———— ————
$^-14$ $^+7$ $^+11$ $^+22$ $^+4$ $^+11$ $^-3$

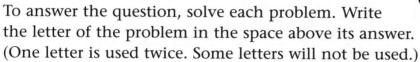

To answer the question, solve each problem. Write the letter of the problem in the space above its answer. (One letter is used twice. Some letters will not be used.)

L. $^+3(^+4 - {}^+5) =$ _____

R. $(^+5 \times {}^+2) \div (^+4 + {}^+1) =$ _____

W. $(^-2 + {}^+3)(^+7) =$ _____

I. $^-2 + {}^+3(^+8) =$ _____

F. $(^-2)^2 =$ _____

P. $(^+3 - {}^+1) \div {}^-2 =$ _____

J. $^+2 - {}^+3 \times {}^+4 + {}^+1 =$ _____

H. $^-(2)^2 =$ _____

N. $^+4 + {}^+4 \div {}^+4 =$ _____

E. $^+2 + {}^+3{}^2 =$ _____

S. $^+7 - {}^+2 \times {}^+4 \div {}^+2 =$ _____

T. $^-(2 + 3)^2 =$ _____

Z. $^-3 \times {}^+4 - {}^+1 \times {}^+2 =$ _____

O. $^-2(^+1 + {}^+4 \times {}^+2) =$ _____

Practice, Practice, Practice! Algebra Readiness   Scholastic Teaching Resources

55

Name _____   Date _____

Going Solo

In 1933, a U.S. pilot made the first solo round-the-world flight. What was this pilot's name?

Answer:

___ ___ ___ ___ ___   ___ ___ ___ ___
1   2   3   4   5   6   7   8   9

To answer the question, find each ordered pair on the diagram. Write the letter of each point in the space above its problem number. (Some letters will not be used.)

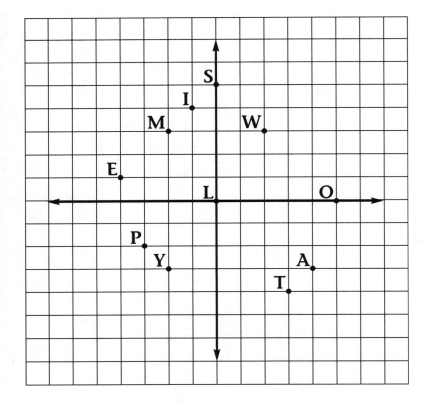

1 (2, 3)

2 (−1, 4)

3 (0, 0)

4 (−4, 1)

5 (−2, −3)

6 (−3, −2)

7 (5, 0)

8 (0, 5)

9 (3, −4)

56

Name _____   Date _____

Let's Go Biking

In 1871, an Englishman built what many historians consider to be the first true bicycle. What was his name?

Answer:

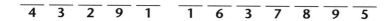

$$\overline{4} \ \ \overline{3} \ \ \overline{2} \ \ \overline{9} \ \ \overline{1} \qquad \overline{1} \ \ \overline{6} \ \ \overline{3} \ \ \overline{7} \ \ \overline{8} \ \ \overline{9} \ \ \overline{5}$$

To answer the question, write the rule above each problem. Find each rule in the Rule Box, then write the letter of each rule in the space above its problem number. (Some letters will be used more than once.)

1 _____

x	y
1	3
2	4
3	5

4 _____

x	y
⁻1	⁻3
0	⁻2
1	⁻1

7 _____

x	y
4	2
2	1
0	0

2 _____

x	y
⁻1	⁻2
0	0
1	2

5 _____

x	y
1	⁻2
2	⁻4
3	⁻6

8 _____

x	y
1	1
2	3
3	5

3 _____

x	y
3	9
4	12
5	15

6 _____

x	y
⁻1	⁻5
0	⁻4
1	⁻3

9 _____

x	y
1	3
2	5
3	7

Rule Box

T. $y = x - 4$

S. $y = x + 2$

Y. $y = {}^{-}2x$

R. $y = \frac{1}{2}x$

M. $y = 2x$

L. $y = 2x - 1$

E. $y = 2x + 1$

A. $y = 3x$

J. $y = x - 2$

Practice, Practice, Practice! Algebra Readiness   Scholastic Teaching Resources

57

Name _____   Date _____

An Inspiring Poem

In 1883, a poem written by Emma Lazarus was inscribed on the base of the Statue of Liberty. The poem expresses the author's belief that the United States is a haven for oppressed people from other lands. What is the name of this poem?

Answer:

" $\overline{}$ $\overline{}$ $\overline{}$ $\overline{}$ $\overline{}$ $\overline{}$ $\overline{}$ $\overline{}$ $\overline{}$ $\overline{}$ $\overline{}$ $\overline{}$ $\overline{}$ $\overline{}$ "
$^{+}16$ $^{-}16$ $^{-}2$ $^{+}9$ $^{-}2$ $^{-}9$ $^{+}6$ $\ 0$ $^{+}1$ $\ 0$ $^{-}13$ $^{-}13$ $^{+}12$ $^{-}13$

To answer the question, evaluate each expression. Use the values of the variables that follow. Write the letter of each expression in the space above its answer. (Some letters will be used more than once. Some letters will not be used.)

$a = {}^-3$ $b = {}^+2$ $c = {}^-4$ $d = {}^-1$ $e = {}^-5$

W. $3a =$ _____

U. $ac =$ _____

R. $ec - b =$ _____

C. $b - c =$ _____

O. $c + d - e =$ _____

I. $d(a + c) =$ _____

S. $a + 2 \times e =$ _____

L. $e \div (c + d) =$ _____

N. $a^2 =$ _____

E. $c - b \div d =$ _____

H. $^-c^2 =$ _____

T. $(e - d)^2 =$ _____

Practice, Practice, Practice! Algebra Readiness   Scholastic Teaching Resources

Answer Key

The First Dinosaur, page 7

1. 9, 11, 13
2. 32, 64, 128
3. 20, 15, 9
4. 21, 26, 31
5. 17, 22, 28
6. 9, 3, 1
7. ●●●, ★★★, ●●●●
8. ★★★●●●, ★★★★●●●, ★★★★●●●●
9. ★★★, ★★★●●●, ★★★★

Answer: Iguanodon

Lady Inventor, page 8

1. 18, 21, 24
2. ★★★, ●●●●, ★★★★
3. ●●, ★★●●, ★★★
4. 8, 13, 21
5. ●●●●, ★★★, ●●●●●
6. 2, 2.25, 2.5
7. 36, 49, 64
8. $\frac{1}{2}$ (or $\frac{5}{10}$), $\frac{2}{5}$, $\frac{3}{10}$

Answer: Mary Kies

"Happy Birthday to You," page 9

E. 11	M. 18
A. 31	L. 41
U. 16	N. 146
R. 8	I. 15
S. 83	K. 132
P. 19	T. 72
D. 69	Y. 7
H. 6	

Answer: Mildred and Patty Hill

Uncle Sam, page 10

L. 2	F. 5
T. 7	S. 84
R. 3	Y. 147
U. 72	A. 6
E. 125	O. 33
M. 12	G. 144
N. 243	J. 168
H. 365	

Answer: James Montgomery Flagg

Wild Weather, page 11

1. 5	11. 23
2. 10	12. 33
3. 15	13. 16
4. 2	14. 21
5. 4	15. 26
6. 8	16. 31
7. 6	17. 18
8. 14	18. 27
9. 30	19. 36
10. 13	20. 45

Answer: Spearfish, South Dakota

A Speedy Flyer, page 12

L. 54	D. 140
U. 8	I. 29
P. 56	E. 336
A. 6	R. 7
F. 147	C. 27
N. 66	W. 72
J. 99	T. 5
S. 4	

Answer: spine-tailed swift

Follow the Signs, page 13

1. −, M	5. −, A
2. ×, A	6. ÷, L
3. ×, U	7. −, O
4. +, N	8. ×, A

Answer: Mauna Loa

A Capital Idea, page 14

A. $n + 3$	E. $n \div 4$
I. $n - 6$	D. $2n + 1$
S. $2n$	C. $4n - 7$
L. $n + 8$	P. $n - 4$
M. $n - 5$	H. $3n - 1$

Answer: Philadelphia

A Very Cold Day, page 15

1. $150 \div n$
2. $n + 25$
3. $3n$
4. $150 - n$
5. $50n$
6. $2n + 3$

Answer: Vostok

Time for Fun, page 16

E. 11	A. 35
M. 21	O. 40
N. 33	R. 3
K. 15	U. 10
C. 0	S. 4
L. 20	P. 6

Answer: Lake Compounce

Iced Tea, Please, page 17

L. 6	I. 10
Y. 5	C. 8
A. 4	R. 12
N. 3	D. 11
H. 7	S. 13
E. 2	B. 1

Answer: Richard Blechynden

Watch Your Step, page 18

U. 18	R. 16
B. 2	A. 4
L. 8	T. 17
W. 3	F. 42
N. 120	S. 56
H. 5	V. 13
E. 26	G. 30
J. 14	Z. 12

Answer: Angel Falls, Venezuela

A Famous Author, page 19

V. $n + 4 = 9$
T. $n - 4 = 9$
L. $n \div 8 = 9$
R. $3n = 9$
P. $(n \div 2) + 5 = 9$
C. $5n - 6 = 9$
N. $3n \div 4 = 9$
A. $3n - 3 = 9$
H. $(n + 4) \div 2 = 9$
E. $3(n + 1) = 9$
S. $(3n + 3) \div 3 = 9$
I. $n(2 + 1) = 9$

Answer: Clive Staples

A Sticky Situation, page 20

L. $16 - 12 = n$

O. $12 - 4 = n$

R. $36 \div 3 = n$

E. $12 + 3 = n$

C. $12 \div 3 = n$

V. $3 \times 12 = n$

Answer: Velcro

A Big Group, page 21

1. A

2. R

3. T

4. H

5. R

6. O

7. P

8. O

9. D

10. S

Answer: arthropods

Ice Cream Cones, page 22

R. 0.7

H. 2.15

L. 1.9

C. 1.63

Y. 3.28

M. 0.899

T. 7.21

S. 0.2

I. 4.57

A. 2.03

O. 8.23

N. 8.8

Answer: Italo Marchiony

Hold on to Your Hat!, page 23

A. 1.26

N. 3.7

R. 3.36

O. 2

G. 318.5

W. 40

H. 1.82

I. 1.7

S. 24.1

U. 1.792

M. 0.3

T. 56.32

Answer: Mount Washington

Exploring Underground, page 24

R. $\frac{7}{9}$

E. $\frac{1}{2}$

B. $\frac{1}{3}$

S. 4

C. $4\frac{1}{2}$

L. $\frac{3}{5}$

N. $\frac{4}{5}$

V. $4\frac{4}{5}$

D. $1\frac{2}{3}$

A. 7

Answer: Carlsbad Caverns

Born on the Fourth of July, page 25

E. $1\frac{1}{7}$

A. $\frac{1}{2}$

I. $\frac{1}{6}$

D. $1\frac{7}{9}$

C. $2\frac{4}{9}$

G. $\frac{5}{6}$

N. $\frac{7}{32}$

L. $8\frac{3}{4}$

V. $4\frac{1}{6}$

O. $3\frac{4}{5}$

Answer: Calvin Coolidge

Grab Your Umbrella, page 26

I. 18.9

O. 73.6

L. 9.3

V. 82.9

U. 6.72

M. 22.24

E. 4.45

S. 4.6

W. 45.78

N. 12.3

T. 57.87

A. 1.82

Answer: Mount Waialeale

Turn on the Radio, page 27

E. 5.22

N. 43.2

R. 0.28

I. 3.8

O. 3

M. 0.004

A. 1.05

U. 71.3

H. 4.68

G. 2.17

L. 3.6

C. 1.6

Answer: Guglielmo Marconi

It's a Gusher!, page 28

I. $\frac{8}{11}$

E. $\frac{5}{9}$

S. $\frac{1}{4}$

U. $\frac{1}{2}$

A. $\frac{14}{15}$

V. $1\frac{1}{4}$

R. $1\frac{5}{8}$

L. $3\frac{7}{10}$

T. 15

Y. $8\frac{3}{4}$

P. $4\frac{3}{5}$

N. $3\frac{1}{3}$

Answer: Titusville, Pennsylvania

Tarzan!, page 29

A. $\frac{2}{3}$

O. $\frac{1}{10}$

I. $\frac{3}{4}$

H. 9

U. $\frac{5}{8}$

G. $\frac{3}{7}$

S. 2

D. $3\frac{1}{3}$

R. $4\frac{3}{4}$

B. $5\frac{3}{5}$

E. $24\frac{1}{2}$

C. $2\frac{1}{2}$

Answer: Edgar Rice Burroughs

Home, Sweet Home, page 30

1. B, 12; I, 13

2. O, 8

3. S, 28; P, 32

4. H, 9

5. E, 10; R, 8

6. E, 3

Answer: biosphere

Time for Reading, page 31

1. S, 1.5

2. A, 7.19

3. L, 3.3

4. I, 0.6202

5. S, 1.2

6. B, 2.9

7. U, 0.96

8. R, 2.4

9. Y, 1.008

Answer: Salisbury

Alive and Well, page 32

1. 8

2. 10

3. 8

4. 81

5. 12

6. 81

7. 25

8. 10

9. 9

10. 9

11. 10

12. 20

13. 15

Answer: fifty trillion

Big Water, page 33

1. 9

2. 16

3. 12

4. 21

5. 49

6. 24

7. 63

8. 15

9. 24

10. 3

11. 16

12. 5

Answer: Lake Michigan

A Wonderful Land, page 34

L. 40

W. 78

G. 9

U. 54

A. 8

D. 72

O. 4.16

E. 52

I. 105

R. 20.16

T. 107.8

S. 26.25

C. 104

N. 62.64

H. 150

Answer: Charles Lutwidge Dodgson

A Presidential Mathematician, page 35

E. 18.24	D. 3.54
A. 88.74	I. 36.32
L. 222.6	J. 50.44
R. 8.91	F. 62.5
U. 22.32	G. 4.75
S. 66	M. 57.8

Answer: James Garfield

Turn Up the Heat, page 36

E. 15%	S. 100%
L. 60%	O. 120%
R. 50%	B. 30%
U. 24%	N. 20%
I. 25%	A. 200%
F. 12%	T. 40%

Answer: International Falls

A First, page 37

L. 100	R. 125
F. 60	D. 84
E. 30	G. 80
Z. 21	I. 55
O. 160	T. 200
N. 40	B. 400

Answer: Gottfried Leibniz

Food for Thought, page 38

R. 135	T. 70
C. 30	I. 60%
N. 160%	O. 800
S. 24	M. 68%
A. 9	

Answer: macaroni

Chips, page 39

S. $3	T. $15
A. 25%	O. 30%
M. $2	L. 5
N. 40%	D. 4%
R. 10	I. $12
B. 12.5%	G. 24%

Answer: Saratoga Chips

Note: Named in part for Saratoga Springs, New York

The Powers of Exponents, page 40

H. 16	P. 64
N. 81	I. 100
E. 343	F. 36
G. 27	C. 32
L. 125	S. 144
M. 256	A. 0
Y. 8	O. 729
D. 243	

Answer: Chinese paddlefish

The Official White House, page 41

L. 26	R. 50
D. 17	T. 85
E. 103	U. 32
H. 9	V. 6
S. 21	W. 0
M. 15	O. 4

Answer: Theodore Roosevelt

The First Vaccine, page 42

1. <, E	7. <, J
2. >, D	8. =, E
3. >, W	9. >, N
4. >, A	10. <, N
5. <, R	11. =, E
6. =, D	12. >, R

Answer: Edward Jenner

A Ride in Space, page 43

1. 7	6. 1.4
2. 5	7. 7.5
3. 8.4	8. 1
4. 8.4	9. 7.1
5. 4.9	10. 3

Answer: Sally K. Ride

Roll the Presses, page 44

H. 400 sq ft	T. 225 sq ft
E. 90 sq ft	M. 135 sq ft
A. 25 sq ft	C. 100 sq ft
U. 300 sq ft	S. 75 sq ft

Answer: Massachusetts

The Biggest Sleepyhead, page 45

S. 60 sq ft	T. 63 sq ft
O. 144 sq ft	K. 48 sq ft
J. 72 sq ft	A. 88 sq ft
R. 12 sq ft	E. 56 sq ft
L. 160 sq ft	

Answer: koala

Pick a Book of Your Choice, page 46

R. 48 sq ft	E. 64 sq ft
O. 88 sq ft	C. 76 sq ft
F. 96 sq ft	N. 121 sq ft
G. 72 sq ft	S. 216 sq ft

Answer: Library of Congress

Sky Gazing, page 47

1. Area = 50.24
   Circumference = 25.12
2. Area = 113.04
   Circumference = 37.68
3. Area = 78.5
   Circumference = 31.4
4. Area = 200.96
   Circumference = 50.24
5. Area = 314
   Circumference = 62.8
6. Area = 615.44
   Circumference = 87.92

Answer: asteroid

What's in the Fridge?, page 48

1. ⁻6, J	6. 0, O
2. 0, O	7. 1, R
3. 3, H	8. 1, R
4. ⁻3, N	9. ⁻1, I
5. 6, G	10. ⁻2, E

Answer: John Gorrie

Fairy Tales, page 49

D. 6	S. 16
E. 8	R. 23
I. 17	U. 15
C. 3	O. 7
P. 14	K. 2
M. 12	G. 62
B. 0	W. 53
A. 5	L. 24
H. 9	J. 54

Answer: Jacob Ludwig Karl, Wilhelm Karl

Big Wings, page 50

1. <, T	10. >, R
2. <, O	11. <, R
3. >, D	12. <, I
4. <, N	13. <, G
5. >, S	14. <, W
6. >, A	15. >, A
7. <, A	16. >, B
8. >, N	17. <, S
9. >, L	18. >, E

Answer: wandering albatross

Play Ball, page 51

1. ⁻5	8. ⁻14
2. 0	9. ⁺15
3. ⁻16	10. ⁻6
4. ⁻9	11. ⁺4
5. 0	12. ⁻14
6. ⁺3	13. ⁻32
7. ⁻13	14. ⁻16

Answer: Boston Pilgrims

Top of the Morning, page 52

1. ⁻5	8. ⁻20
2. 0	9. ⁺16
3. ⁻16	10. ⁻21
4. ⁺2	11. ⁻3
5. ⁻20	12. ⁻23
6. ⁻15	13. ⁺2
7. ⁺16	

Answer: Mount Katahdin

The First Video Game, page 53

1. ⁺28	9. ⁻18
2. ⁻12	10. ⁺40
3. ⁺27	11. ⁻9
4. ⁻15	12. ⁻4
5. ⁻12	13. ⁻18
6. ⁻4	14. ⁻15
7. ⁺81	15. ⁺10
8. ⁺17	

Answer: Magnavox, "Odyssey"

A Presidential Pet, page 54

1. ⁻16	9. 0
2. ⁻22	10. ⁺11
3. ⁺12	11. ⁻2
4. 0	12. ⁺16
5. ⁻4	13. ⁻9
6. ⁻18	14. ⁺18
7. ⁻4	15. ⁺20
8. ⁻20	

Answer: goat, Old Whiskers

Model White House, page 55

L. ⁻3	R. 2
W. 7	I. 22
F. 4	P. ⁻1
J. ⁻9	H. ⁻4
N. 5	E. 11
S. 3	T. ⁻25
Z. ⁻14	O. ⁻18

Answer: John Zweifel

Going Solo, page 56

1. W	6. P
2. I	7. O
3. L	8. S
4. E	9. T
5. Y	

Answer: Wiley Post

Let's Go Biking, page 57

1. $y = x + 2$	6. $y = x - 4$
2. $y = 2x$	7. $y = \frac{1}{2}x$
3. $y = 3x$	8. $y = 2x - 1$
4. $y = x - 2$	9. $y = 2x + 1$
5. $y = -2x$	

Answer: James Starley

An Inspiring Poem, page 58

W. ⁻9	S. ⁻13
U. 12	L. 1
R. 18	N. 9
C. 6	E. ⁻2
O. 0	H. ⁻16
I. 7	T. 16

Answer: "The New Colossus"

Notes

Notes